The subject matter and
vocabulary have been selected
with exp...   ...e
brief and ...   ...d
in large, ...

Children's questions are
anticipated and facts presented
in a logical sequence. Where
possible, the books show
what happened in the past
and what is relevant today.

Special artwork has been
commissioned to set a standard
rarely seen in books for this
reading age and at this price.

Full-colour illustrations are on
all 48 pages to give maximum
impact and provide the
extra enrichment that is the
aim of all Ladybird Leaders.

A Ladybird Leader

roads

written by James Webster

illustrated by Gerald Witcomb, Martin Aitchison
and Roger Hall

Publishers: Ladybird Books Ltd . Loughborough
© Ladybird Books Ltd 1974
Printed in England

Stone Age Man

Early men were hunters.
They did not need roads.
They just followed the animals
which they hunted.

The first tracks

Later they began to farm
and lived in villages.

There were tracks between the villages.

Roman roads

Soldiers could not march quickly
on rough tracks.

The Romans made roads of stone.

These were long and straight.

The Roman roads were very well made.
They were used for hundreds of years.
After the Romans, no good roads
were made for a long time.

7

A road 300 years ago

Three hundred years ago
there were still no good roads.

Coaches stuck in the mud.
They often turned over.

Roads and robbers

Coaches were often stopped by robbers.

Rich people had to hand over
their money and jewels.

It was dangerous to go far by road.

Roads for cars

When the car was invented,
roads were still narrow and rough.
Now there are many cars and trucks.
Modern roads must be wide
and smooth.

Making a modern road

To make our smooth, wide roads,
big machines are used.
They do the work of many men.
This bulldozer moves earth and trees.

15

This machine scrapes
and levels the ground.
Unwanted soil is removed by it
and dropped where needed.

One man can work this big machine.
It is 32 feet 6 inches (9.906 m) long
and weighs 26,900 lbs (12 201 kg).

This truck is being filled with stones at a quarry.
A road is built on a layer of stones.

This machine picks up the stones
at the quarry.

It loads them quickly
into the truck.

A mixture of stones and hot tar
is tipped from a truck
in front of this machine.

The machine spreads and levels it
to make the road smooth.

Modern roads and robbers

Cars can move fast on modern roads.
Robbers can get away more quickly.
This makes them harder to catch.

Old roads and modern traffic

Cars cannot move fast
on old, narrow roads.

Sometimes there is not room
for two cars to pass.

Roads over mountains

Roads over hills and mountains
must twist and turn.

Then they are not so steep.

If the road was straight,
it would be much shorter.

But it would be too steep
for cars to climb.

This road does not twist and turn.
It is very steep.

The car and caravan
will not reach the top.

A road high over water

This is Sydney Harbour Bridge
in Australia.
The road on it is 170 feet (51.816 m)
above the water.
A railway runs beside the road.

A road that can be raised

Here is Tower Bridge in London.
The road over it is in two parts.
The parts rise to let ships pass under.

A road train

Road trains like this carry cattle in Australia.

They are used on the road from Alice Springs to Darwin.

This road is nearly 1,000 miles (1 609.34 km) long.

Some of these trucks
have sixteen forward gears.
Most of them have ten forward gears.

Another long road

This road crosses Canada.
It is the Trans-Canada Highway.

The picture shows it
near the Rocky Mountains.

A road in a cold country

In very cold countries, snow and ice can cover the roads.

Cars like this are sometimes used.

A road in a hot country

Roads across deserts are often tracks
over the sand.

They are used by camels
as well as cars.

A road in an eastern country

This is a road in the East.

Rickshaws are part of the traffic.

Some are pedalled like bicycles.

Others are pulled by men running.

A road in Holland

Because Holland is so flat,
many people ride bicycles.

Paying to use a road in Italy

In some countries, drivers must pay
to go on a motorway.

This helps to pay the cost
of the motorway.

Paying to use a bridge in Britain

Sometimes drivers must pay
to cross bridges.

On this bridge, they pay
to cross the River Severn.

Roads can be blocked by Nature

Trees, rocks, floods and snow
can block roads.
Sometimes deep snow
can cover a car.

When roads are flooded,
cars must be driven slowly.
The car will stop
if water gets in the engine.

Keeping roads clear

This road is in Norway.
Rocks may fall on it.
Wooden barriers hold back rocks
and snow.

Roads can be blocked by man

This building is a Customs Post. Passports, luggage and goods must be checked when leaving and entering a country.

Roads need repairs

Even modern roads
sometimes have to be repaired.
Road repairs hold up traffic.

In towns, there are water pipes,
gas pipes, electric cables
and drains under the roads.

Sometimes these must be repaired.

Road racing

Sometimes a road is used for racing.
When this happens, other traffic
must not use it.

Roads use up land

Every year there is more traffic
on the roads.
More and more good land is used
for roads.

Land used for roads
can no longer grow crops for food.
More food, not less, is needed.
Each year, millions more people
must be fed.

Roadsides

Sometimes the sides of roads
are sprayed to kill weeds.

But this also kills many wild flowers,
insects and birds.

Many birds, insects and small animals need hedges for shelter.

Some roadside hedges, like this one, are cut too low.

Some are even pulled out.

Then there is less wild life.

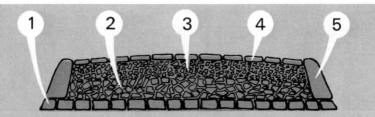

A Roman road

1 Stone blocks
2 Rubble
3 A layer of broken tiles or bricks
4 Top paving
5 Kerbstones

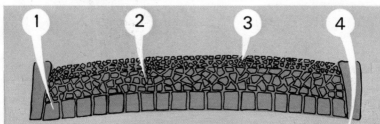

A Telford road

1 Heavy flat stones
2 A layer of broken stones
3 A top layer of smaller stones or gravel
4 Earth